Darker Sh

Michael Punter's work for the theatre includes *The Wolves* for Paines Plough (short-listed for the George Devine and Margaret Ramsay Awards), *The Birds* (after Aristophanes) for Birmingham Rep, *Dummy* and *The Nightwatch* (Margaret Ramsay Award) for Pop-Up and *Upstart Crows* for The Young Pleasance Company (Edinburgh Festival). He has recently adapted *The Mark of the Horse Lord*, from Rosemary Sutcliff's novel, for the National Theatre Studio, along with the short play *nationaltheatre*, which was produced last year to celebrate the National Theatre's Student Day. His work for BBC Radio includes *Come to Me* and *The Glad House*. He is currently Visiting Lecturer in Drama and Theatre at Royal Holloway, University of London.

Michael Punter

Darker Shores

Methuen Drama

Published by Methuen Drama 2009

1 3 5 7 9 10 8 6 4 2

Methuen Drama
A & C Black Publishers Ltd
36 Soho Square
London W1D 3QY
www.methuendrama.com

Copyright © Michael Punter 2009

Michael Punter has asserted his rights under
the Copyright, Designs and Patents Act 1988 to be identified
as the author of this work

ISBN 978 1 408 12831 2

A CIP catalogue record for this book is available
from the British Library

Typeset by Country Setting, Kingsdown, Kent
Printed and bound in Great Britain by
Good News Press Ltd, Ongar, Essex

Darker Shores

A Ghost Story

For Will and Manny,
and also for Lisa, their beautiful mum

Darker Shores premiered at the Hampstead Theatre, London, on 3 December 2009. The cast was as follows:

Stokes	Mark Gatiss
Mrs Hinchcliffe	Pamela Miles
Beauregard	Julian Rhind-Tutt
Florence	Vinette Robinson

Director Anthony Clark
Designer Paul Farnsworth
Lighting Designer Tim Mitchell
Video and Projection Designer Thomas Gray for The Gray Circle
Sound Designer Edward Lewis

Characters

Gabriel Stokes, *a naturalist, mid-forties*
Florence Kennedy, *a housemaid, mixed race (white/Afro-Caribbean), twenties*
Agnes Hinchcliffe, *a housekeeper, fifties*
Tom Beauregard, *a spiritualist, American (from Virginia), thirties*

The Apparition

Place

The offices of Tom Beauregard, Covent Garden, London.
The Sea House, on a desolate stretch of the East Sussex coast.

Time

December 1875, December 1876.

The play is written so that The Apparition, the flood and other
manifestations of the haunting can be produced by a number
of means: physical performance, data/digital projection, or
a combination of these. This would honour the tradition of
Pepper's Ghost.

Act One

In the dark, a child sings 'I Saw Three Ships', distant, fading as lights come up on . . .

Covent Garden, London. A room in the offices of **Tom Beauregard.** *Well-stocked bookshelves, furniture of fine quality. Two chairs, with a low table between them. A Christmas tree. A yellowish light from outside, traces of a fog. It is late afternoon.*

Professor **Gabriel Stokes** *is frozen in the mid-point of exclamation. He searches for a way forward but cannot find one.*

A clock ticks. Dull clop of traffic beyond.

Beauregard   Professor?

Beat.

Professor Stokes, are you able to proceed?

Beat.

Can you say the word, Professor?

He goes to a cabinet, retrieving a bottle of whisky and two tumblers. He sets them down.

Tennessee. I hope the New World does not offend. In the years after the Civil War, it was all my countrymen had left. That and their horses, and the rags they stood up in. Not that I saw any action myself. Shall I pour?

Stokes (*finally*)   No. No, not for me. I don't.

Beauregard   The Good Book informs us 'a little wine is good – '

He smiles and pours.

Stokes (*covering his tumbler*) No. No, that won't be necessary.

Beat. The clock ticks on.

Beauregard   If it's any consolation, Professor, men such as yourself – brilliant men, men of influence and position – oftentimes find it hardest to say the word –

Stokes   What word?

Beauregard   'Haunting'.

Stokes   Is that what is happening to me, Mr Beauregard?

Beauregard   It's *Doctor* Beauregard.

Stokes   May I enquire as to the provenance of your doctorate? The University of South West Chickamauga, formerly the Spiritualist Church of Chatanooga – ?

Beauregard   It's true. I'm not a Fellow of King's College Cambridge. But nor am I some colonial dunce. And, at present, truth to tell, you need my help.

Stokes   True. (*Without contrition.*) I apologise.

Beauregard   I am a trance medium. Clairvoyant and clairaudient. Would it be impolite to enquire where you heard of me?

Stokes   A friend. A friend of a colleague had seen you at a – (*an effort*) seance . . . in Paris. You gave information about his late aunt that, he believes, you could not have discovered by any regular means.

Beauregard   Ah. I do recall the case. Yes.

Beat.

Stokes   It's important to remember that I am, first and foremost, a man of science, Dr Beauregard. A natural historian. I live and breathe the unlettered past. The moments after that brooding spirit passed over the face of the waters . . .

Beauregard   As I was going on to say, men of such stature oftentimes find it hardest to accept –

Stokes   The outrageous. The irrational. The *impossible*.

Beauregard   The *extraordinary*. That which presently rests beyond our science.

Stokes   Dr Beauregard, consider this.

He takes out a small apple and places it between them.

Bought in the market this afternoon.

Beauregard An apple.

Stokes Source of our first great unhappiness.

Beauregard Very well.

Stokes Sir, how can we be certain that this *exists*?

Beauregard *picks up the apple. Weighs it.*

Stokes The evidence of our senses?

Beauregard I suppose so . . .

Stokes *takes the apple.*

Stokes Let's say some cataclysm stripped us of our sight. Then our smell. Then our taste and then our touch −

Beauregard (*smiling*) My. You have truly considered this, Professor −

Stokes Would this apple exist to you? Would it? And, therefore, does it, Dr Beauregard? (*He sits forward, urgent, agitated.*) Does it *exist* at all?

He holds up the apple.

Beauregard It exists, sir. It exists. There must be demonstrations. Proofs . . .

Stokes This hypothetical cataclysm has taken our world away.

Beauregard Except it has not.

He drinks. **Stokes** *resets the apple.*

Beat.

Stokes That question has troubled me since I could first think. Indeed, I believed it to be the most troubling thought I could experience. Until I came to The Sea House. What happened to me in that house, Dr Beauregard, I cannot explain. Cannot rationalise. Cannot comprehend.

Beat.

Beauregard   I can help you.

Stokes   Can you?

Beauregard   I believe that I can. But I must know the facts of the case so far.

Stokes   Facts. Yes. 'The Facts of the Incident at The Sea House.' Yes.

Beauregard   Please begin.

Stokes *hesitates. Begins. As he does so,* **Beauregard** *writes occasional notes.*

Stokes   I had known of the place since childhood. A magnificent house on a promontory, stranded on the easternmost edge of Sussex. A nearby church of Saxon origin fell into the sea some time ago. Evidence, the locals say, of the power of the forces that reside in that strange and melancholy corner of the world. The house itself had been built by a former officer in the army of the Duke of Wellington, a man named Darlish. He had attempted to create a magnificent garden of flora and fauna from across the Empire. But the English weather did for that.

Beauregard (*looking to the window*)   I can quite imagine. And yet one must admire the grandeur of his folly.

Stokes   Indeed. A new Eden upon a blasted shore.

Beauregard   No wonder you were drawn to it.

Stokes   But there were rumours. That Darlish had sought ways to prolong his life beyond its natural allowance. Ancient ritual, even human sacrifice, were spoken of. Darlish eventually hanged himself from the bough of an oak, which revealed a conservatism somewhat at odds with his florid reputation. When I was sent away to school, The Sea House was put up for sale and fell into disrepair . . .

Beauregard   So how did you come to rediscover it?

Stokes   A friend of mine in London had become
acquainted with a missionary, a man of apocryphal zeal who
had blazed his way across the Indian subcontinent. He had
acquired the place, then vanished from the face of the earth
some years ago. All rather mysterious, and leaving the great
house empty, save for his housekeeper, Mrs Hinchcliffe. A
woman bright with portents, but dark of facts . . .

*The world of The Sea House has slowly come to life behind them.
Ghostly at first, and then more solid.* **Mrs Hinchcliffe** *can be seen,
carefully arranging flowers.*

Stokes *moves from his seat and leaves the room, moving around the
house.* **Beauregard,** *when he speaks, continues to address his empty
chair as though he were there.*

Stokes   The house itself had the strangest atmosphere of
any I had ever visited. There was a . . . perpetual scent . . . not
simply of flowers . . . but of something else. Was it mint . . .
or camphor? The room that was to be mine was large, with a
commodious table for my books, specimens and the typewriter
that would produce, I had cause to hope, my masterpiece. I
felt . . . (*great surprise*) joyful

Beauregard   Is it so unusual to be joyful, sir?

Stokes   I am a communing member of the Church of
England. Any species of happiness is a downright miracle, sir.

Beauregard   I see.

Stokes'*s luggage is already there. We see more of the room now,
including a number of statues, draped with dustsheets. A fire comes to life
in a grate.*

Stokes   My room was on the first floor of the house. And
before I proceed with my narrative, I should inform you of
the view from the west-facing window. For it was quite
extraordinary. One could see, with the tide at bay, across a
vast landscape of shingle. This was punctuated by dark rivers
of water, and outcrops of rock that resembled primordial
men, stranded in some terrible instance of supplication, yet
transformed by a beautifully clear light into . . . something

else. The impression was of a world in a constant state of flux and occasional tumult. It was magnificent. Holy. Beautiful . . .

Beauregard   And so it regained its hold upon your imagination.

Stokes   It did. But I understood perfectly the nature of my experience. My reverie . . . was something *other*, and understood as such. Had the other window been accessible, the east-facing window, the view across the water would have been even greater – the effect . . . of being in some great lighthouse, in the midst of the sea itself . . .

Mrs Hinchcliffe *has arranged the flowers.*

Mrs Hinchcliffe   A good journey, Professor Stokes?

Stokes   Somewhat trying, Mrs Hinchcliffe. The Hastings train did not run according to Bradshaw, and the luncheon was unsatisfactory. The connection to Rye was lost due to a sheep on the line, whose solitary plight occupied the Southern Railway men for the best part of three quarters of an hour. She had lost her lamb, which was duly located bleating its way across the marsh. The news of this was met with a round of applause from the frustrated passengers. The cab from Rye was lively but not entirely perilous. And I must confess that, now I am here, the reward more than compensates for the effort expended. There's such an overpowering sense of . . . quiet.

Mrs Hinchcliffe   We're a peaceful lot, sir. Not a great deal happens, truth be told. And that's how we like it here.

Stokes   And that is how I shall like it, Mrs Hinchcliffe.

Mrs Hinchcliffe   There are many good walks to be taken, sir. The coastal paths afford some lovely views.

Stokes   I shall on occasion be working late into the night. Is that likely to be a problem?

Mrs Hinchcliffe   This part of the house is yours, sir. There's only myself on the other side, and the girl who does for me. She has private quarters.

Stokes   And there is a floor above?

Half-beat.

Mrs Hinchcliffe   An attic, sir. The master used that for his . . . nick-nacks.

Stokes   The master?

Mrs Hinchcliffe   The owner of the house, sir.

Stokes   Of course. The missionary. He vanished off the face of the –

He senses he has overstepped the mark.

I'm sorry, Mrs Hinchcliffe.

Mrs Hinchcliffe   We live with it, sir.

Stokes (*a gesture*)   You know, I don't think I have known a grander room!

Mrs Hinchcliffe   The master liked it. He had little cause to leave it.

Stokes   His name, I take it, is still upon the deeds of the house?

Mrs Hinchcliffe   I believe so, sir.

Stokes   Would it be impolite to ask how you're managing to live?

Mrs Hinchcliffe   Visitors, such as yourself. I hope to make the place a hotel, what with the railway and all.

Stokes   Well, you keep the place beautifully. Were the master ever to return –

Mrs Hinchcliffe   He will not return, sir.

Stokes *moves to the rear, which is heavily curtained.*

Stokes   And this area is . . .

He is about to look . . .

Mrs Hinchcliffe   A terrace, sir. The master loved his terrace. He would . . . look out . . . on summer days. The inside of

a house like this . . . can be stifling in such weather. We leave
it as it was. To honour him.

Stokes   So there is no access?

Mrs Hinchcliffe   It's as described in the list of particulars,
sir.

Stokes   His predecessor had quite a collection of flora,
I believe –

Mrs Hinchcliffe (*abrupt*)   Before my time, sir. You may
breakfast as late as you like. Evening meals are by arrangement,
but the girl can soon lay out a cold collation. Will that be all?

Stokes   Thank you. Yes.

Mrs Hinchcliffe *goes.*

Beauregard   So much for your new Eden, Professor! But
there was little to trouble you thus far.

Stokes   True. Save for . . .

*He stands before the largest covered statue. He raises the dust sheet and
looks beneath without revealing it.*

St Francis of Assisi.

Beauregard   And what was he doing?

Stokes   Healing the sick. But the image was neither
comforting nor inspirational. And the others . . .

*He lifts the other dust sheets in turn, again without revealing what is
beneath.*

Stokes   A cherub. And a Pan, sticking his tongue out.
Perhaps from the collection of Darlish and left to honour him.

He lowers the dust sheets.

Beauregard   And that is all?

Stokes   That is all.

The stage darkens slowly.

Stokes   I have come to find the Christmas season particularly hard in recent years. And so, with some alacrity, I set about recreating my study at King's. Unpacking books, papers, the stuff that would aid in the creation of a masterpiece . . . Finally . . . the aforementioned *typewriter*! A miraculous invention, and my one truly indispensable possession.

He sets his typewriter upon the desk, then disappears behind a screen.

Beauregard   May I ask what is the nature of the book you are writing?

Stokes (*calls*)   Certainly. It's to be called *A Rebuttal and Refutation of the Fraud Charles Darwin, his Origin of Species and Lie of Natural Selection.*

Beauregard   Oh . . .

Stokes   I take it you have read his work?

Beauregard   No, sir. But I am aware of its content.

Stokes*'s clothes are flung over the screen as he speaks.*

Stokes   Mr Darwin would have it that we are the godless children of apes.

Beauregard   I understand that's the meaning of it.

Stokes   Then if it is so, pray tell me this: chimpanzees are still procreating. Why has one not given birth to a man of late?

Beauregard   You know, there's a pastor in my village in West Virginia who'd cheer that sentiment to the rafters, Professor.

Stokes   And he shall soon have a written defence, sir!

He emerges in his nightshirt and takes his place at his desk. He feeds paper into the typewriter.

It has long been my habit to work late into the night. A window had been left open, and I did not close it. I have some tolerance for cold, as my late wife often pointed out . . .

Beauregard   I assumed you were a bachelor, Professor.

Stokes   No. I should sooner say that word than the one I dread: *widower.*

Beauregard   My condolences. How long?

Stokes   Fifteen years. Almost to the day.

Beauregard   Children?

Stokes   A son. They were lost together. The sinking of the S.S. *Heroic* in the Atlantic, 24 December 1860.

Beauregard   I'm sorry.

Beat.

Stokes *types.*

Stokes   I settled down to work as usual. And yet my opening chapter was obstructed by a troubling question. (*He stops typing*) It was this: did Adam, our biblical father, possess an umbilicus?

Beauregard   Excuse me?

Stokes   A navel. A belly-button. In brief, had Adam been bound to someone? Or something. Had Adam ever been a child? Perplexed, I took to my bed.

He gets into bed, extinguishing a lamp before doing so. He closes his eyes. Sea sound, distant.

And then it began.

A whispering, within the sea sound. Something calling.

Yes. Of course it is the sea. A friend once told me that the coast is as noisy as Piccadilly, if one's ear is tuned right . . . My ear . . . was becoming so attuned . . .

The whispers again.

But there it was. Unmistakable. Something within the sea sound. Speaking. Speaking to me. But I would shut it out . . .

He turns over in bed, pulling the blankets tight.

Beat.

Beauregard   I take it that was not the end.

Stokes   No. No, it was not.

Beat.

Upon the second night, at the same time, the noise above began.

Above, the sound of something being dragged.

Over and over. Something . . . rolling . . . something being dragged along, was it?

The sound over and over.

Until it stopped.

Beat.

Then began again.

Beauregard   How long?

Stokes   Minutes? An hour?

Beauregard   What did you do?

Stokes *(calls)*   Will you stop, will you please stop?

Beat.

And then there was nothing but the sea again.

He rises from the bed. Goes behind the screen. Light. Birdsong. Morning.

Beauregard   And that was all?

Stokes   Oh, believe me, there is more to come.

Beauregard   Did you consider at this point the supernatural?

Stokes   Of course not. I am a natural historian. Inspired by faith. The only supernatural events I know of are – *(quick, perfunctory)* the conception of a boychild by a spotless virgin; the miraculous works of that boychild; his subsequent victory over the grave via the cross, and final ascension to His Father in Heaven.

Beauregard   I see.

He looks out from behind the screen.

Stokes   I do not believe in the supernatural, Dr Beauregard.

Beauregard   And yet you could not explain these sounds.

Stokes   But it does not follow that they were *inexplicable.*

He emerges, dressed rather sportily, and moves the typewriter.

The following morning I had kippers.

Mrs Hinchcliffe *appears and presents the breakfast.*

Stokes   But I had little appetite for them.

Mrs Hinchcliffe   The breakfast isn't to your liking, sir?

Stokes   Mrs Hinchcliffe, does my room suffer . . . a problem with draughts?

Mrs Hinchcliffe   Not to my knowledge, sir. I know it's your pleasure to leave the window open a bit.

Stokes   No, it's not that.

Mrs Hinchcliffe   Then I've no report of draughts.

Stokes (*to* **Beauregard**)   I was beginning to wonder how my predecessor had managed.

Mrs Hinchcliffe   Would you favour a poached egg, then?

Stokes   What about rats?

Mrs Hinchcliffe   Sir!

Stokes   I mean, in the attic above. Might there be . . . could there be . . .

Mrs Hinchcliffe   On my word, sir, I never heard of such a thing in my house! Rats? Vermin! Here?

Beauregard   It sounds as though she would have had you pack your bags.

Stokes   Indeed. At that point, I wished the ground beneath might open and swallow me up.

Mrs Hinchcliffe   Beg pardon, sir, but this is a clean house. It's ever such a clean house. Ask around. Ask anywhere. The whole village. They'll tell you what a clean house this is.

She turns and goes. She is close to tears.

Stokes (*calls*)   Mrs Hinchcliffe! Please! I meant no harm!

He rises and leaves the table. Puts on shoes. Locates a golf bag. As he does so:

I thought it best to take myself away for the day. It had been nothing, I was sure. The wind. The creaking and settling of an old house in winter. I took to the golf course.

Light change. Clouds. **Stokes** *has retrieved a putter and is weighing it up.*

In addition to the destruction of the unconscienable Darwin, I had another, darker, purpose to my visit: the improvement of my short game on one of the county's wilder courses. And I was quite alone. Not a single living soul appeared to observe me. I have grown accustomed to solitude, and perhaps even cherish it. Yet, upon that dark December day, I yearned for something – for conversation . . . someone to talk through what I had seen – what I had *perceived*, at least, in that house . . . And then, as though my wish had been granted by some strange agency, there was . . . someone . . .

Florence *enters. She is dressed for the cold, a muffler tight to her face. She holds a balloon. She does not notice* **Stokes**. *She is waiting. Agitated . . .*

Stokes *looks, trying to catch her eye. Thinks again. Doesn't want to frighten her. Putts the ball a short length. Cannot contain himself.*

Stokes   Hello!

Florence *turns.*

Stokes   Are you . . . do you . . . are you lost?

Beauregard   And was she lost? Was she lost, Professor?

Stokes   She was . . . what I believe you might term . . . a *mulatto*.

Beauregard   A negress?

Stokes   No. Not entirely. A mulatto.

Beauregard   You spoke to her?

Stokes   I attempted to. (*To* **Florence.**) Hello? Do you speak English? (*Louder.*) Eng-lish? (*He jabs a finger towards her.*) *Parlez-vous Français?* I'm staying up at The Sea House. The Sea House. *Ici je rest* – Ah.

She has gone.

Beauregard   And she was real?

Stokes   She held a balloon!

Beauregard   A balloon?

Stokes   Yes! I'd quite forgotten the balloon . . .

Beauregard   But, for a moment, you considered her to be . . . a ghost.

Stokes   She was very much flesh and blood. As I was soon to discover.

Uneasy, he packs away his putter and sets the bag aside.

Beauregard   I am intrigued, Professor. *Flesh and blood!*

Stokes   She was . . . is . . . a *fact*, sir. She exists. As I hope I have made clear, I am a man of science and also a man of faith. They have nothing to fear from each other. Nothing at all to fear.

He returns to the chair in **Beauregard***'s office. Picks up the apple. The house darkens.*

Stokes   A loving God sustains this world and all things in it. Our *Father*, who art in Heaven.

Pause.

Beauregard   Yet, did not the Greeks believe the universe to be made up of imperceptible particles? Realities within realities. I am simply attempting to shed some light, Professor.

Stokes *replaces the apple.*

Stokes   Beauregard, you are a 'spiritualist'.

Beauregard   A Doctor of the *Spiritual Science* –

Stokes   Then you are familiar, I take it, with the work of Mrs Betty Hoop? Mrs Hoop, a so-called 'spirit medium', was preparing a shopping list at her home in Highgate last spring when she, quite against her will, dematerialised, only to reappear moments later upon a tabletop in Holborn, in the midst of a 'seance'. Mrs Hoop is quite living, and weighs in excess of twenty-two stones. She destroyed the table and near crippled the poor woman whose parlour it was. The last words upon Mrs Hoop's shopping list were ' . . . and two pounds of Lincolnshire sausages'. So reported the London *Times* on the 21 April 1874.

Beauregard   What offends you more? The theatricals or the fact your favourite newspaper reported it?

Stokes (*furious*)   Both, sir! Mrs Hoop was never in Highgate! She was concealed, Lord knows how, somewhere within the room, perhaps within a 'spirit chamber', or perhaps in the voluminous crinolines of an *even larger lady*!

He has been banging the table. He becomes aware of this and calms himself.

Beauregard   They're fraudulent mediums, sir, not Russian dolls –

Stokes   I cannot be drawn into this world of . . . superstition!

Beauregard   Then I ask again: why are you here, Professor?

Stokes *moves back into the room.*

Stokes   For an answer.

Half-beat. **Stokes** *rises and moves away from the chair. He places his typewriter and the house reawakens.*

Beauregard   You are sure there were no other occupants of the house?

Stokes   There were none. As the sun set, I felt uneasy. I dined, then set about my work. (*He sits.*) There was no storm. No spiteful sea to unsettle me. I determined to work through the night, to concentrate my mind upon my great project. I put aside the troubling matter of Adam's umbilicus, until –

The sound begins again, a dragging from above.

It was not entirely oppressive until . . .

The sound changes to a thumping, as though somebody were punching the boards.

WILL YOU STOP IT FOR THE LOVE OF GOD!

The sound stops. Then the dragging, louder, heavier.

THIS IS INTOLERABLE, I HAVE MY WORK, I –

He throws open the door stage left and discovers **Florence**, *ascending the stairs to the attic. Her arms are full of toys, which she drops in surprise.*

Beauregard   Who? Who did you discover?

Stokes   The mulatto.

Beauregard   The negress?

Stokes   The same. I could not contain myself. And, I am ashamed to say, I was not quite the gentleman . . .

He has seized **Florence**, *near-throwing her over the threshold into the room. She falls to the floor, spilling the remainder of the toys.*

Beauregard   And what did she say?

Stokes   Nothing. We gazed upon each other as though each had fallen from some distant star.

Beat.

Florence   Sir?

Stokes   Madam!

Florence   Sir!

Stokes   From the golf course!

Florence   I'm the housemaid, sir –

Stokes   Did you not consider . . . at this hour . . .

Florence   Please, sir . . .

Stokes   The dragging and the banging and –

Florence   I did nothing of the kind, sir.

Stokes   You made some considerable noise, madam!

Florence   Sir, I was returning these things to the attic. My son . . . plays here.

Stokes   Mrs Hinchcliffe did not mention a child.

Florence   He . . . visits . . .

Stokes   She does not know!

Florence   It's my only chance to see him, sir. Please don't tell, sir. She won't allow him here, she –

Beat.

You have a child, too.

Stokes   What? *What?*

Florence   Nothing, sir. Sorry, sir.

Neither knows quite what to say.

Stokes (*resuming*)   Look, it is your affair, Miss –

Florence   Kennedy, sir. Florence Kennedy.

Stokes (*ruefully*)   Irish.

Florence   I'm a Londoner, sir.

Stokes   Well, I'll thank you to stop entertaining the child so late.

Florence   He's in his bed, sir. Please don't tell. My mother brings him. She'll collect him tomorrow. When I saw you, I was awaiting them . . .

Stokes   But the sound . . . the dragging –

Florence   He's barely five years old, sir.

Stokes   Five years – But you heard the sounds . . . you *made* the sounds.

Florence   Sir, I didn't make any sounds.

Stokes   You and the boy were playing. It's the only explanation . . .

Florence   The attic is quite empty sir!

Footsteps, running, above.

Stokes   There. The boy is running.

Florence   Sir, my son is in his bed. Mrs Hinchcliffe is in her bed. The only ones awake are . . .

Stokes   You and I.

The next sound is a barrage of noise, an assault, a hammering all around the room.

The lamplight flickers. Goes out. Dark.

Oh sweet God . . .

Florence   What is that?

Stokes   It's . . . all around us . . .

Florence   Find the light! Please, sir!

They are becoming increasingly desperate . . .

Stokes *gropes for the lamp. Lights it.*

Stokes   Here. It's here!

Florence   Sir, keep it close. Don't let it go out!

The hammering is still all around them, a constant, uneven drumming . . .

Stokes   I shall speak to Mrs Hinchcliffe about this. Mark my words –

And then it stops.

The wind blows softly, moving the curtains.

Florence   It's over.

Stokes   I shall be raising a number of points . . . perhaps . . . requesting a refund for tonight –

Then a soft tapping is heard.

Florence   What is it? What is that?

Stokes   It's it's . . . coming from . . .

He gestures towards the curtains.

Florence   The terrace, sir!

Stokes   Somebody . . . wishes to come in . . .

The tapping, more insistent now. He edges towards the curtains.

Somebody is having some sport with us, Miss Kennedy. Somebody is enjoying themselves at our expense . . . but it ends . . .

He is standing by the curtain rope.

NOW!

He pulls on the rope, the curtains part, revealing large windows. The terrace behind is partially lit by moonlight. We see the glass is obscured.

Silence.

Great relief from both.

It's the wind. Things . . . out on the terrace . . .

Florence   The master's old things!

Stokes   Not a ghost. Not a spirit.

Florence   Maybe a bird! Gulls . . .

Stokes   Perhaps . . . it's possible to step out. To take the night air.

He tries the door, also glass. It is locked.

Key.

He looks at the foot of the door, sweeping his hand along the floor. Finally, he raises the lantern to the glass again. As he does so, we see a figure. The **Apparition***, obscured, stares at him.*

Stokes *sees and starts.*

Florence *sees and starts.*

The **Apparition** *is moving across the glass, tapping and scraping. He seems to follow them.*

Stokes *drops the lantern in panic. He and* **Florence** *run to the door stage left. They pull on it, kick at it. But it will not open.*

The **Apparition** *stares at them. He moves to the door. Taps, scrapes. The handle is tried.*

Stokes *and* **Florence** *hold each other.*

Stokes   WHAT DO YOU WANT IN THE NAME OF GOD, WHAT DO YOU WANT WITH US?

Blackout on the house. Lights on **Beauregard***'s office.* **Stokes** *remains in his position, holding* **Florence***. A lamp flickers back to life in the house.*

Stokes   And what word would you use to describe this?

Beauregard   I would use the word 'haunting'.

Slowly, a beautiful dawn light comes up on the house. Reddish, wintry.

Stokes   We remained for hours. She slept. A sleep of nightmares. I could feel her trembling, her heart racing. I had not been close to . . . to anyone . . . since my wife . . . and to . . . to feel her was some comfort . . . the warmth of her . . . her breathing . . . I admit it was exhilarating. We had faced something terrible together. And I do not doubt that it meant us harm . . . that *thing.* It wanted . . . I don't know what it wanted . . . I would say that it wanted to claim our very souls –

Beauregard   But you don't believe in the supernatural.

Stokes   No. I do not.

With some effort, he lifts **Florence** *on to the bed.*

Stokes   I knew her story to be true. She had no part of this.

Beauregard   Are you quite sure?

Stokes   Quite sure.

Beauregard   Because such phenomena are, in my experience, usually associated with women or children.

Stokes   She had no part of it.

He is gazing at **Florence**. *He moves to touch her hair. Hesitates. As he does so . . .*

Stokes   It has nothing to do with her at all.

Beauregard   Professor Stokes.

Stokes *carries on, a reverie.*

Beauregard   Professor Stokes!

Stokes   Yes, what?

Beauregard   There is no straightforward answer to your problem. So I propose a visit.

Stokes *returns to his chair in* **Beauregard**'s *office. The house darkens again.*

Stokes   You will come to The Sea House?

Beauregard   I have certain matters to attend to tomorrow morning. So I propose we meet at Charing Cross station, beneath the clock, at ten minutes to two, ready for the coastal train upon the hour.

Stokes   Sir . . . now I have told you . . . I am not entirely convinced that I am able to return . . .

Beauregard   You shall return. We shall get to the heart of this.

He picks up the apple.

My fee is thirty guineas. Excluding expenses.

Stokes   Thirty!

Beauregard   Half in advance.

Stokes   Very well.

Beauregard *holds up the apple.*

Beauregard   There may be illusion in this, Professor.

He makes the apple disappear.

Stokes   Good Lord –

Beauregard   But you have my word, whatever has passed in that house, we shall come upon the truth.

He makes the apple appear again.

Blackout.

The distant singing of 'I Saw Three Ships' again. Fading . . .

The Sea House. The room. We see the curtain has been restored. A birdcage, also covered, sits upon the floor and, nearby, a bucket of hot water and brushes. Beside them lies a bag.

Mrs Hinchcliffe *reads from a small Bible, closely examining the text. She reads aloud, softly, faltering occasionally . . .*

Mrs Hinchcliffe   'Then shall the priest command to take for him that is to be cleansed two birds alive and clean, and cedar wood, and scarlet, and hyssop . . . And the priest shall command . . . shall command . . . that one of the birds . . . be killed in an earthen vessel over running water . . . '

She lifts the cover of the cage. Some chatter within.

There. Don't be sad, pretties. Don't be sad now . . .

From the bag, she takes out a small knife, a vessel and cuttings from plants. She reads on:

'And as for the living bird . . . he shall take it . . . and the cedar wood . . . and the scarlet and the hyssop . . . and shall dip them and the living bird in the blood of the bird that was killed – ' Oh, good God. I can't . . .

A knock at the door. She hides the Bible, knife and other items. Hangs the bird cage. Returns to the brushes and water and scrubs.

Florence *enters, understandably hesitant. She carries flowers.*

Florence   Where do you want them, ma'am?

Mrs Hinchcliffe   On the desk there.

Florence *places the flowers.*

Florence   Are the birds . . . to stay?

Mrs Hinchcliffe   They are.

She scrubs.

Florence   Ma'am, when are we to decorate?

Mrs Hinchcliffe   Decorate what?

Florence   For Christmas, ma'am! I've picked some holly and little Caleb has made some stars –

Mrs Hinchcliffe   Save it for your quarters, Florence.

Florence   But ma'am –

Mrs Hinchcliffe   Idols, girl. Pagan idols. Should get rid . . .

She gestures to the statues. Shakes her head.

Florence (*sotto*)   Bah, humbug!

Mrs Hinchcliffe   What?

Florence   Nothing.

Beat.

He asked about the master.

Mrs Hinchcliffe *stops work.*

Mrs Hinchcliffe   Then tell him all you know.

Florence   I don't know anything.

Mrs Hinchcliffe   There.

Florence   But I saw . . . something –

Mrs Hinchcliffe   Will you hush!

Half-beat.

Florence   Professor Stokes asked. In the village . . . people ask . . .

Mrs Hinchcliffe   Listen, you stupid child. There are some things best left. Things that can harm.

Florence   Harm?

Mrs Hinchcliffe   Be warned. Don't speak of him.

Beat.

Florence   Ma'am, what about Caleb?

Mrs Hinchcliffe   Enough!

Half-beat.

Florence   Might he stay Christmas night? Just this once –

Mrs Hinchcliffe   Do you really wish to bring a child here now? Have you thought of the harm it might do?

Florence   No.

Half-beat.

Mrs Hinchcliffe   Then work and be glad.

As the lights fade on them, they come up on the stairway. A commotion as **Stokes** *and* **Beauregard** *ascend the stairs with baggage.* **Stokes** *is unsettled, clearly very nervous. He fumbles for a key.*

Beauregard   . . . and I saw something similar in Jasper, Georgia, Professor. A curious episode. One night, the father of the house, a respectable man who'd managed gangs on the southern railroads before the Civil War, took an axe from his woodshed, entered the house where his family were at their prayers and, giving no impression whatsoever of what was to come, he –

The key is found and very quickly used.

Stokes   We're in.

Beauregard   Ah. Good.

Lights on the room as they enter. A large chair has been placed with blankets and a sheet folded carefully upon the seat. **Beauregard** *moves to the window casement.*

You were right about the view. My God. And the rocks . . . like people . . . how did you put it?

Stokes   'Stranded in some terrible instance of supplication.'

Beauregard   Absolutely. Absolutely.

Stokes   It is an extraordinary place.

Beauregard *stands before the large statue. He lifts the dust sheet.*

Beauregard   Oh my –

Stokes   St Francis of Assisi.

Beauregard   Ah! But wasn't he kindly?

Stokes   I assume they belonged to Darlish.

Beauregard   Yes. Our immortal Eden-ite.

He lowers the dust sheet. Meanwhile **Stokes** *is beside the east window, pawing the curtain hesitantly.*

Stokes   She's restored the curtain.

Beauregard *joins him.*

Stokes   And what have we here?

Stokes *looks into the birdcage. The birds stir.* **Beauregard** *goes to the curtain.*

Beauregard   So. Shall we do the honours?

Stokes   I . . . we . . .

Beauregard   You're afraid?

Stokes   As you should be.

Beauregard   I'm a spiritualist, Professor. I know what to expect.

Stokes   I hope you do. *I hope you do.*

Beauregard   And what is that smell?

Stokes   Yes. It is remarkable. I thought it camphor.

Beauregard   Is it?

Stokes   No. Something else . . .

Mrs Hinchcliffe *is at the door. She knocks.*

Stokes   Step away. For a moment.

They do so.

Enter.

Mrs Hinchcliffe *enters.*

Mrs Hinchcliffe   Is all to your liking, sirs?

Stokes   Yes, thank you, Mrs Hinchcliffe.

Beauregard (*bowing*)   Merry Christmas.

Mrs Hinchcliffe (*correcting*)   *Advent*, sir. We await the Saviour at this time. He is not yet present among us. We wait. In the dark. For His coming.

Beauregard   Yes. Of course. My mistake.

Beat.

Mrs Hinchcliffe   You're an American gentleman.

Beauregard   Guilty as charged!

Stokes   Thomas is my . . . um . . . cousin. From Virginia. I don't think you were introduced downstairs . . .

Mrs Hinchcliffe   I've aired a room, if you'd like.

Beauregard   Please don't put yourself to any trouble. I shall only be staying a night or two. To help my . . . cousin.

Stokes   I need Tom's expertise. Mostly on the golf course. My short game is . . . it's . . .

Beauregard   It needs a lot of work.

Beat.

Mrs Hinchcliffe (*careful, considered*)   I'm very sorry if you were inconvenienced the other night, sir. I've had Mr Stone, the builder, have a look at the roof. He thinks it might have been the tiles. Some are loose. He's going to strip it down in the summer, sir.

Stokes   An expensive business for the householder.

Beauregard   An expensive business for you, Mrs Hinchcliffe.

Mrs Hinchcliffe   I'm not the householder, sir.

Beauregard   But you are. According to the Land Registry.

Beat.

Mrs Hinchcliffe   No, sir. The master was never declared deceased.

Beauregard   But he was. There was no body. But the court in Calcutta declared it overwhelmingly likely that he was dead. Cause unknown.

Mrs Hinchcliffe   Sirs, I trust you'll have a good stay –

Beauregard   You own The Sea House, Mrs Hinchcliffe. The master having no living issue. Isn't that the truth?

Stokes (*sotto*)   Steady on, Beauregard.

Beauregard   Isn't that the truth of the matter, Mrs Hinchcliffe? Special dispensation was sought in the courts of law.

Beat.

Mrs Hinchcliffe   It's true, sir. I own it.

Beauregard   Then why hide it?

Mrs Hinchcliffe   It is a private matter, sir.

Beauregard   A remarkable thing. A woman of property who is not titled.

Mrs Hinchcliffe   It was . . . the master's wish . . .

Beauregard   What was he to you?

Mrs Hinchcliffe   I . . . assisted him . . . in his work . . . here in the house . . .

Stokes (*sotto*)   Look here, Beauregard, the woman's clearly upset −

Beauregard (*sotto*)   It's not my intention to upset her. Merely to get to the heart of this −

Stokes (*sotto*)   You think this is relevant?

Beauregard (*sotto*)   I don't yet know whether or not The Sea House is haunted, Professor. But I believe that an atmosphere of secrecy can make such places as this . . . vulnerable . . .

Stokes (*sotto*)   Vulnerable? A *place*? Vulnerable?

Mrs Hinchcliffe   Sirs. The matter is private. The matter is closed. There's supper at seven, sir. Florence will attend to you.

She rushes from the room.

Stokes   Was that really necessary?

Beauregard *pulls back the curtain. We see the large windows and doors of the terrace. The glass is obscured, marked and badly weathered. Shapes of objects visible beyond, clouds scudding fast above.*

Beauregard   There. Some light upon the matter.

Stokes   What's happened to the glass? It looks . . . scarred.

Beauregard   The wind carries sand and salt. Seen it in the Carolinas, too. What's beyond?

Stokes   A staircase. Locked. Iron gates.

Beauregard   The master's name was Marchant.

He moves around the room.

Elijah Marchant. A self-made man.

Stokes   I fear he did something terrible, sir.

Beauregard   There was a firm, Marchant and Son, importing cotton, before he gave it up for God.

Stokes   But what kind of god?

Beauregard   One might well ask.

Stokes *sits.*

Stokes   Marchant and *Son*?

Beauregard   That's right.

Stokes (*considering*)   *No living issue* −

Beauregard *is now trying the terrace door. It will not yield.*

Beauregard   Help me.

Stokes *moves to help.*

Beauregard   It hardly moves. How long has it . . . ?

The door will not relent.

Stokes (*smiling*)   Curiouser and curiouser . . .

Beauregard   What's that?

Stokes (*fondly*)   From a book about a girl. Name of Alice. My son used to −

Beauregard   You said there was noise from above?

Stokes   I believed it was the housemaid's boy.

Beauregard   And you're sure it was not?

Stokes   Quite sure. She was as terrified as I was. She − I felt her heartbeat . . .

Beauregard (*smiling*)   *Flesh and blood*, Professor.

Stokes   Look here, I hope you aren't suggesting I −

Beauregard   I'm not suggesting anything. But the negress can be a veritable Nefertiti . . .

Stokes   Who?

Beauregard A Queen of Egypt.

Stokes I don't believe your people treated the negroes like royalty, sir.

Beauregard *takes offence.*

Beauregard I'll have you know that I fought for the Union in the war. Sir.

Stokes You claimed before that you did not fight. In your office. When you first poured me a drink. You said –

Beauregard I saw a little action. Briefly. Before I realised my folly.

Stokes You deserted?

Beauregard No. I simply did not re-enlist. (*Turning.*) And Mrs Hinchcliffe claims there's no key for this door?

Stokes Lost, she says.

Beauregard Convenient.

Florence *has been listening at the door for some moments. She knocks.*

Beauregard Come in.

Florence *enters. Awkwardness in* **Stokes**.

Florence Sirs, tea will be served shortly in the drawing room.

Stokes Th-thank you.

Beauregard Hello, Florence.

Stokes Ah. Forgive me. This is –

Beauregard Tom Beauregard, Florence.

Florence (*cool*) Sir.

Beauregard (*sotto, to* **Stokes**) You were right. Nerfertiti.

Florence Sir?

Beauregard 'The beautiful woman has come.'

Stokes   What?

Beauregard   The meaning of the name. In Egyptian.

Florence   I'm from Bermondsey, sir.

Beauregard   Can you tell me what you saw here?

Florence   Professor Stokes saw it too, sir.

Beauregard   But what did *you* see?

Florence *shifts, uncomfortable.*

Florence   I saw a figure at the glass. A man.

Beauregard   Young or old?

Florence   I don't know.

Beauregard   Did it mean you harm?

Florence   I think it did.

Beauregard   I believe you have a son, too.

Florence   I do, sir.

Beauregard   His name?

Florence   Caleb, sir. Kennedy.

Beauregard   Caleb. And Caleb exists?

Stokes   Beauregard!

Florence   He exists.

Beauregard   Not a . . . figment? Not a phantom?

Florence   No, sir.

Beauregard   Then may we see him?

Florence   He cannot stay here. It would . . . bring shame for Mrs Hinchcliffe, sir.

Beauregard   But you *have* brought him here. In secret.

Florence   Sir –

Beauregard   You told Professor Stokes –

Florence (*to* **Stokes**)   Sir!

Stokes   That will be all, Florence. Thank you.

Florence   Thank you, sirs.

She goes, crestfallen.

Beat.

Stokes   That was distasteful.

Beauregard   All must be tested, Professor.

Stokes   And how do you propose to proceed?

Beauregard   We'll begin tonight.

Stokes   How? A seance?

Beauregard   An investigation. I do believe our tea is getting cold.

He makes to go.

Stokes   I know what I saw.

Beauregard   Let's take tea. Then you can walk me around that golf course. All will be well, Professor.

He goes.

Stokes   I hope you're right. (*Sotto.*) Good God, I hope you're right.

He follows, happy to leave the room.

Beat.

For a moment, we see the **Apparition** *at the window. He places a hand upon the glass.*

Blackout.

Act Two

Evening of the same day. Light up on the house. In the room, **Beauregard** *lights candles in preparation for the seance. The curtains are undrawn, exposing the glass.* **Stokes** *paces nervously, reading a book. The fire flickers. Upon the landing,* **Mrs Hinchcliffe** *and* **Florence** *are gathered by the door, listening.*

Mrs Hinchcliffe   Did you clean?

Florence   I did.

Mrs Hinchcliffe   And the birds?

Florence   Fed and watered.

Mrs Hinchcliffe   Good. That's good.

A distant singing of 'I Saw Three Ships' by a small group. Hearty, but not entirely in tune.

Florence   Carollers.

Mrs Hinchcliffe   It isn't Christmas!

Florence   Christmas Eve tomorrow, ma'am.

Mrs Hinchcliffe   *Advent!*

Florence   Shall I give them something?

Mrs Hinchcliffe   Thick ear.

Florence   Mince pie? I made some. Forgive me –

Mrs Hinchcliffe   Go on.

Florence *goes.*

Beat.

Mrs Hinchcliffe (*a quiet prayer*)   Be at peace. Please. No more of this. It's done. Be at peace now.

She goes.

Beauregard *is now covering a table with a dark green cloth. Chairs are placed.* **Stokes** *sets his book aside and takes his seat.*

Stokes   Is this theatricality really necessary?

Beauregard   It's to soothe the mind, Professor. Nothing more.

Stokes   Don't see why it can't be done in broad daylight.

He looks under the table.

Beauregard   There are no tricks, Professor. The table will not cavort about the room.

Stokes (*attempting levity*)   You are not Mrs Betty Hoop of the voluminous crinoline!

Beauregard   This is a science, sir. The spiritual *science*.

Stokes   But why must it happen at night?

Beauregard   When did you see this figure?

Stokes   At night.

Beauregard   There.

Stokes   But why should these spirits not visit at noon?

Beauregard   Sometimes they do. There's a woman back home who sees Thomas Jefferson at lunch every Tuesday.

Stokes   Really?

Beauregard   She sets her clock by him.

He lights the final candles.

Stokes (*attempting levity again*)   I say, a friend of mine at King's asked me this the other week, 'Why don't the working classes see ghosts?'

Beauregard *ignores this.*

Stokes   Why don't the working classes see ghosts?

Beauregard *again ignores this.*

Stokes   Because they're too busy!

He laughs.

Stokes   Too busy! Ha!

Beauregard   Now, before we begin, I'm going to ask you to clear your mind of −

Stokes *is sniffing the air.*

Stokes   Is it me, or is the air even sweeter?

Beauregard   I haven't noticed.

Stokes   Sweetness. Terrific sweetness! And it's not camphor. No, something else. (*Sniffs.*) Hyssop! That's it! She uses hyssop to clean −

Beauregard   What is hyssop?

Stokes   It's a herb. Its name comes from Hebrew − *ezob*, meaning 'holy herb'. Pliny the Elder refers to it in his *Natural History* −

He reaches for the book again. **Beauregard** *sits.*

Beauregard   Let us begin.

Stokes   It was used to purify. (*Leafing through the book.*) And for sacrifice . . .

Beauregard *clears his throat.* **Stokes** *takes the hint.*

Beauregard   You will note that the table is a table. I have made no adjustments or additions . . .

Stokes   It is a table. (*Patting it.*) A common or garden table.

With a slight flourish, **Beauregard** *produces from his bag a small, wooden effigy, bird-like.*

Stokes   And what's that?

Beauregard   Something from the Indians near my home, Professor.

Stokes   Now look here. I will not countenance shamanism!

Beauregard   To concentrate the mind, Professor. It has no other value.

Stokes   Good. For I have no interest whatsoever in tribal dancing, ritual or any attendant warbling, sir!

Beauregard   You go to church, don't you?

Stokes   That is different!

Beauregard   Please try to keep an open mind.

He places an apple upon the table.

Stokes   Your point?

Beauregard   Whatever should happen to us, it exists. Correct?

Stokes   It exists.

Beauregard   How do we know?

Stokes   We perceive it. Here and now. *Agree* upon it –

Beauregard   Please relax. Place your hands palms down on the table.

Stokes *does so.*

Beauregard   And breathe deeply, regularly.

Beat.

And now we may begin.

Beat.

Is anyone there?

Beat. The birds are chirruping in their cage.

You entities who have no corporeal existence . . . speak! Please speak! Make yourselves known to us. Now.

The candles flicker.

Stokes   Good Lord . . .

Beauregard   If you are present, please show yourselves.

Silence.

Stokes   Well, that appears to conclude our business, Dr Beauregard. Thank you so much for your time.

Beauregard (*joy*)   You're here!

Stokes (*fumbling*)   You have had a cash advance and the remainder shall be a cheque drawn on my Coutts' account –

But **Beauregard** *appears deep in a trance. He looks beyond* **Stokes** *to a point by the stage-left door.*

Beauregard (*not to* **Stokes**)   Yes. I understand.

Stokes   I take it a cheque is accepta –

Beauregard (*to* **Stokes**)   They are both here.

Stokes   Who is here? And where?

Beauregard   Look at them!

Stokes   Where?

The candles flicker again. Unseen by both men, the dust sheets slip from the statues. A sigh from **Beauregard***.*

Beauregard   Welcome, madam.

Stokes (*whisper*)   What am I looking for exactly?

Beauregard   And you, young man! Well, aren't you just charming?

Stokes   Dr Beauregard!

Beauregard   Your name is . . . Bertie!

Beat.

Stokes   *Now look here* –

Beauregard   Bertie really misses his daddy.

Stokes   Beauregard, don't –

Beauregard   And Bertie is handsome. He is quite the young gentleman!

Beat.

He wants to look for treasure by the sea again . . .

Stokes   What?

Beauregard   And spot birds from the hide at Hun . . . stanton.

Stokes   Hunstanton!

Beauregard   Ice cream on the pier there!

Stokes   Oh God. Oh, my boy . . .

He strains to see. He is frantic.

What am I looking at? *Is he here?*

Beauregard (*to the spirit*)   You are welcome, madam.

Stokes   Who? Where are they?

Beauregard   Please. Come to me. Now –

His head snaps back.

Stokes   No! Beauregard!

Beauregard *relaxes. Another persona is now speaking, a cultivated, English voice. Female.*

Beauregard   Hello, Gabriel.

Stokes   You . . . are . . . Who are you?

Beauregard   It's Elizabeth, Gabriel.

Stokes   Elizabeth?

Beauregard   Your Elizabeth! Bertie and I are well. Think of this, my darling, as a great tour or adventure. It will make it so much easier. We are both in the light. We felt no pain. And so many of our dear friends are here. Bertie runs and plays in the light, darling, you should see him –

Stokes   Elizabeth?

Beauregard   Yes, my darling?

Stokes   Why are you using the name you hate?

Beauregard   My . . . love?

Stokes   You are Bess! You were always Bess! Your father called you Elizabeth. You hated him, so hated the name.

Beauregard   I . . . Gabriel . . .

Stokes *stands, furious, overturning his chair in the process.*

Stokes   FRAUD! UNCONSCIENABLE FRAUD! SHAME ON YOU!

He yells, chokes, sobs.

Beauregard *still seems entranced.*

Beauregard   What . . . what . . . are you doing?

Stokes   You have been to the Public Records Office! You have read the newspapers! You *knew* they were lost on the *Heroic*!

Beauregard   No –

Stokes   My articles in *The Naturalist* describe an ornithological hide at Cromer, *close to Hunstanton* –

Beauregard   Professor –

Stokes   You *knew*!

Beauregard   I did not know!

Stokes   FRAUD!

Beauregard   No, sir – What's that sound?

It has already begun, quiet at first, then rising, the sound of a storm at sea. It grows and continues to grow . . .

My God, what is that?

Stokes   Is this you? Your work!

All light is extinguished. The storm reaches a shattering intensity. Within it, several voices, including a woman and a child:

Voices   God!

Save us! Save us –

The Lord is my Shepherd –

Please –

I shall not want –

I'll give anything. Please!

He maketh me.

It's coming –

He maketh me –

The wave –

Please God, no –

To lie down –

No –

In green pastures –

NO!

Stokes *stands within the storm, daring it. Confronting it.*

Stokes   Bess! Bess! I'm here! BESS!

The crashing of a great wave. As it hits . . .

BERTIE!

The sound subsides. Darkness.

Silence for a time.

Then some birdsong, then some morning light.

Both men are revealed curled up, shivering, in the centre of the room. Upon the stage lies a lifebelt bearing the name 'Heroic'. A length of rope is attached, with a frayed end. It has been in the water for a considerable time.

But the apple remains where it was put.

Beauregard *lifts himself up on his elbows. Collapses. Tries again. Collapses.*

Stokes   How . . . are . . . you?

Beat.

Beauregard   What?

Stokes   How . . . are you?

Beauregard *laughs briefly. He sees the lifebelt.*

Beauregard   What is that?

He lifts himself and struggles over to it.

Stokes   A lifebelt from the S.S. *Heroic.*

Beauregard   Now do you believe?

Stokes   Believe what?

Beauregard   We were on the deck of that ship!

Stokes   Were we?

Beauregard   You cried out to your wife!

Stokes   An illusion. Of superlative quality but –

Beauregard   Professor!

Stokes   – an illusion, nonetheless.

Beauregard   How?

Stokes   You are a fraud, sir. An illusionist – *(he points to the apple)* as you have demonstrated, who used the time before coming here wisely –

Beauregard   Your wife and son were here!

Stokes   Our clothes are quite dry, sir! This room is unchanged, save for us!

Beat.

Even Betty Hoop, of the voluminous crinoline can *research*, sir! You visited the Public Records Office. You also stopped off at the library.

Beauregard   *There* is the lifebelt of a ship –

Stokes   A prop. A theatrical's prop.

Beauregard   And the storm? You have a cause for the storm?

Stokes   A ruse. Perhaps you mesmerised me. That's it! You have spent time in France, sir! Home of mesmerism and mob rule! Darwin would pay much to see me humiliated!

Beauregard   I think you overestimate your own significance.

Stokes   I fight for God, sir. And the world he *made*, and the creatures and objects – apples – he populated that world *with*. A kind God, sir. A God who would never willfully *deceive* or take away the means to apprehend *His* creation –

He is overcome by emotion. Contains it. It's all he has ever done.

He sits.

Beat.

Forgive me.

Beat.

Beauregard (*with quiet purpose*)   Your boy was five years old. Your wife was visiting her oldest friend, married to an American. You did not want her to leave, for storm clouds were gathering in my country then. You quarrelled. But you loved her to distraction. You kissed them both at the dockside and made them promise they'd be home for Christmas. You hugged your son and held him close to you. He said: 'I won't let you go.' And to you, that was sunlight. For he had changed you. Made you certain, for the first time, of an order in things. You had something to work for. Something to defend. You loved him more than your own life, and you thought the time before him to be but a pale and empty dream. He was living itself to you, wasn't he, Professor? And, since he was torn away from the deck of that ship, you have felt nothing at all. For anyone or anything.

Beat.

Stokes   What parent does not love their child, uncritically and without condition? I lost my son. A fact I cannot alter.

Cannot change nor redeem. My consolation is that he was
with his mother, who loved him as I did. Men love their wives.
Parents love their children, one hopes. That is no revelation,
Dr Beauregard. Your 'gift', if it might be called that, is a sort
of vague intuition, empathy teamed with a rum sort of luck.
I could see it at the Egyptian Hall in Piccadilly on any night,
save Sunday, paying no more than one penny.

Beat.

Beauregard   Professor, the gift is not constant, and I confess
that I have, on occasion, assisted the spirits somewhat in their
manifestations –

Stokes *guffaws.*

Beauregard   Yes. I did know of your wife and son. But
they still stood before me as real as you are now.

Stokes   Your words may give comfort to the simple-minded –

Beauregard   This is no *comfort*, Professor! You cannot deny
the evidence of your senses. Here.

He throws the lifebelt at **Stokes**.

Beauregard   It exists. Another world.

A knock at the door. Both start.

Sweet Jesus!

Stokes   Who is it?

Florence (*brightly*)   Me. Florence. Early morning tea, sirs?

Stokes   Come in.

Florence *comes in, deftly holding the tray. She looks at the two men.
Almost drops the tray.*

Florence   I'm sorry, sirs. Forgive me but – Oh, God in
Heaven . . .

She points to the lifebelt.

What's that?

Beauregard   It is the lifebelt of the *Heroic*.

Florence   The ship that sank?

Beauregard   The ship that sank.

Stokes   Drowning my wife and child. Fifteen years ago this very day.

He pushes the lifebelt away.

Florence   Oh, sir. I'm so sorry. But . . . how is it here?

Beauregard   According to the Professor, I have mesmerised him.

Stokes   You have not. I accept that.

Florence   Mesmerised?

Beauregard (*fear into elation*)   So you concede? You concede that this is evidence of the supernatural?

Stokes   I came to defeat Darwin, sir. Not to overturn the Enlightenment.

Beauregard   But you cannot explain this?

Stokes   Alas, sir, I concede that I cannot.

Beauregard   HA! Good!

He begins to gather his things.

Stokes   What are you doing?

Beauregard   Leaving.

Stokes   What?

Beauregard   There will be no further charge, Professor.

Florence   Sir, this spirit must be confronted.

Beauregard   So you are an expert now, Miss Kennedy?

Florence   You know it must be done.

Beat.

Beauregard   But not by me. I have discovered America. Others may subdue it. Good day to you both. It has been illuminating.

He is at the stage-left door when:

Stokes   COWARD!

Beat.

Beauregard   What did you say?

Stokes   You heard me.

Beauregard   Don't say that. Don't ever say that.

Stokes   Why? You fled the war and you are fleeing this house. Coward!

Beauregard   I would strongly advise you to retract that remark.

Stokes   And if you fought for the Yankee Union, sir, then I am a Dutchman!

Beauregard   Retract, sir! Or else –

Stokes   I am a naturalist. I call a thing by its name. The swallow. The cedar. The duck-billed platypus. You, sir, are a COWARD!

Beauregard *moves aggressively towards* **Stokes**.

Florence   Sirs! Think of the mistress. I beg you!

Beauregard   You do not know one half of it, sir!

He turns, taking out money. He throws it at **Stokes**.

Beauregard   *Take back thy accursed money!*

He goes, slamming the door.

Beat.

Stokes *stands.*

Stokes   Forgive me, Florence, for that altercation. I –

He collapses.

Florence   Sir, the mistress has brandy.

Stokes   No. I cannot. Thank you. If you could . . .

Florence *helps him to a chair.*

Stokes   How does she live with this?

Florence   Before you came, there were . . . instances. Noises.

Stokes   But nothing to match a tempest in a room?

Florence   No.

Stokes   Is it me?

Florence   I don't know, sir.

Stokes   Have I summoned it here?

Florence   How?

Beat.

Stokes   My loss. My grief.

Florence   I don't know.

Stokes   My *rage*?

Florence   I wish I could tell you.

Beat. **Stokes** *composes himself, embarrassed. Smiles.*

Stokes   Curiouser and curiouser.

Florence (*smiling*)   *Alice's Adventures in Wonderland*, sir.

Stokes   You know it!

Florence   My son insists upon it every bedtime.

Stokes   It's full of madmen, is it not?

Florence   It's a paradise! Tea?

Stokes   Tea? Yes!

Florence *pours tea. As she does so:*

Florence   'Once upon a time there were three little sisters, and they lived at the bottom of a treacle well.'

Stokes   What?

Florence   'What did they live on?' (*She places his cup.*) 'Treacle!'

Stokes   What are you talking about?

Florence   The Dormouse, sir!

Stokes (*smiling weakly*)   Yes . . . yes, very good.

Florence   Sorry.

Stokes   No. I'm grateful. Um –

Florence   Milk and sugar?

Stokes   Please. Two, please.

They drink for a moment.

Florence   That man, Mr Carroll, sir, he sees like a child. How big the world is. How frightening and exciting it is. We've forgotten, but he remembers just what it's like, to be as free as a child. My Caleb has a chapter every night. And when he's finished, he has it again.

Stokes   Does he often visit you here?

Florence   Sometimes. Mrs Hinchcliffe won't have him in the house. At first, I thought it was our colour, but it's not that. She has faith, sir. I give her that. Often says how a black man carried Our Lord's cross.

Stokes   And Caleb . . . has no father?

Florence   He does, sir. But we hardly see him. I know him from the village. The first house I was in service, he delivered for the greengrocer. He asked me if I wanted to go dancing and . . . well . . . one thing led to another and . . . when I told him, he looked like he'd seen a ghost. Beg pardon, sir. He fled back to London and that was that. Mrs Hinchcliffe took me on soon after. No one else would've touched us. She's kind like that, sir. A godly woman. That first time you saw me, I was waiting for Caleb. I'd got him a balloon from those gypsies camped at Winchelsea. He lost it later and he got all cross.

She sips tea.

I can't do without him, sir. It's a weakness with me.

Stokes   Would that more people had such a weakness, Florence.

Florence   Thank you, sir.

Both drink for a moment.

He inhales.

Stokes   Why does Mrs Hinchcliffe use hyssop?

Florence   She says it keeps things clean.

Stokes   Many things might do that. She said the master, Elijah Marchant, went to the East.

Florence   He vanished there.

Half-beat. A thought.

Stokes   What if he didn't?

Florence   What do you mean?

Stokes   Perhaps she has hyssop because Marchant *returned* with it. He returned from the East! Where else would she have got it? Florence, I don't think he vanished at all. I think he returned. I think he is in this house!

He is now on his feet, pacing.

Florence   Sir, you've taken a turn . . .

Stokes   We know what sort of man he was! A fanatic! A firebrand! Perhaps he is testing us. Testing our faith. Using us – Such a house as this could conceal a man. Within its rooms, its grounds . . . And if he is here, then I shall find him!

He makes quickly for the stage-left door.

Stokes Stay here, Florence!

He leaves.

Florence *is alone. She looks around the room. Begins, half-heartedly, to tidy.*

She goes to the birdcage. Opens the door. The birds are dead.

Florence Oh, sweethearts. Poor little things . . .

She cradles the birds. Replaces them in the cage.

She draws back the curtain. A sky of winter clouds. Some snowfall. The terrace in shape and outline.

We see a balloon tethered on the terrace. It sways.

She sees the balloon. She tries the door to the terrace. For the first time, it opens. She passes through the door. It shuts behind her. We now see her in shape only. She moves to untie the balloon. Flurries of snow are in the air. Then:

A gull shrieks. **Florence** *turns towards it, stage right. The shriek is sustained, amplified, echoing as the* **Apparition** *enters from stage left, moving at speed. He sweeps her off, stage right, in a single movement. It is over so quickly that we might doubt that it happens at all.*

The balloon floats away.

Blackout.

The golf course. Snow still in the air. A seat.

Beauregard *sits alone, clutching his suitcase.*

He sets it down. He is shaking.

Mrs Hinchcliffe *approaches.*

Mrs Hinchcliffe Do you mind if I . . .

Beauregard Go ahead.

She sits. They stare out to sea.

Mrs Hinchcliffe   I like to watch the ships here.

Beat.

I think I'd like America. I'd like the sky.

Beauregard   How so?

Mrs Hinchcliffe   I saw a show about it at the Alhambra, years back. They put a ship upon the stage. A beautiful clipper in full sail. Lovely big painted clouds beyond. It was set before that war you had.

Beauregard   Yes. That war we had.

Mrs Hinchcliffe   What was that all about?

Beauregard   I have not the faintest idea.

Beat.

Mrs Hinchcliffe   Steamers took the place of clippers. Give me a sail any day. Progress they call it. What's progress? My dad was a weaver. Worked the loom at home with us crawling and toddling. Factories came and first day he lost his finger. We were half starved. What progress is that? What does it *mean*, any of it?

Beauregard   I really do not know, Mrs Hinchcliffe.

Beat.

Mrs Hinchcliffe   Look, I told a lie about the house. But I'm not a *liar.*

Beat.

It's a clean house, sir.

Beauregard   Yes, you have said –

Mrs Hinchcliffe   It's ever such a clean house.

Beauregard   Madam, I have never encountered in all my time such raw, such *elemental* power from the world of spirit as I discovered today in your home. I very much doubt that it can be *cleansed.*

Beat.

Mrs Hinchcliffe   Well, there's not a lot I can do about that.

She folds her arms.

Beat.

It knows me. It's content with me. It only gets upset –

Beauregard   When?

Mrs Hinchcliffe   When others come.

Beauregard   I admire your fortitude, Mrs Hinchcliffe.

Mrs Hinchcliffe   Are you leaving?

Beauregard   I must.

Mrs Hinchcliffe   You'll miss the last train from Hastings.

Beauregard   Then I'll get a hotel.

Mrs Hinchcliffe   On Christmas Eve? Our Saviour couldn't find a place on Christmas Eve.

Beauregard   Then at least I am in good company. Goodbye.

He makes to rise.

Mrs Hinchcliffe   Don't go. Please. Stay . . .

Half-beat.

Beauregard   I cannot.

Mrs Hinchcliffe   Run, then! If that's who you are! If you've no *backbone*!

A beat. **Beauregard** *does not move.*

Beauregard   Have you ever heard of Gettysburg?

Mrs Hinchcliffe   Can't say I have.

Beauregard   The last great battle of the Civil War. Maybe the worst there's ever been. And I was there. A kid out of his depth, in Confederate grey. The losing side, you may have heard. The ones who wanted to keep the blacks enslaved. But some of us fought for other things. The right to preserve our patch of earth. Home and hearth. So there I was, no shoes and with the world on fire. They gathered us recruits together and marched us at the Yankee lines. And we walked. We opened up our guns and theirs fell silent. We marched on. And we got so close we could almost *touch* those Yankee guns! I recall, at my shoulder, Jeb Smith of Concord, Tennessee, turning and grinning. (*He hesitates.*) Grinning as the shot took away his chest and left him standing. Spine, ribs. Still grinning. You see, those Yankee guns weren't done. Could you endure that? I did not. I turned and ran, and the ranks parted before me. I *ran*, through orchards hung with corpses. If there is a God, he had not favoured us at Gettysburg. That night, I ran some more. Into the forests of Pennsylvania. And there *I saw Jeb Smith again*! As real as before. Holding his arms out to me and beckoning me to another world. And I've been looking for that world ever since. In halls and seance rooms. Far from home. But the dead, I have found, are every bit as inconstant as the living.

Beat.

Mrs Hinchcliffe   I'm sorry. For what I said.

Beat.

You think the master is haunting us?

Beauregard   I believe he is a malignant, fallen soul . . .

Mrs Hinchcliffe   No! He was a good man, sir. He was the holiest man I ever met –

Beauregard   I believe that you know more than you will ever tell.

Mrs Hinchcliffe   It's not him. Can't be him . . .

Beauregard   Mrs Hinchcliffe, I confess I cannot return to that house now. I do not know what happened to that man Marchant and I do not wish to know –

He rises.

Mrs Hinchcliffe   I'll tell you all the same.

Beauregard   Please. Please do not.

Mrs Hinchcliffe   The master came home from his travels, sir. But he came home a leper.

Beat.

Beauregard   Oh Jesus . . .

Mrs Hinchcliffe   And I think the disease is still in the house. In the walls and floorboards. He was a leper, and he died screaming here! Sealed away. Destroyed. But he went to give comfort!

Beauregard   So you clean. You purify . . .

Mrs Hinchcliffe   I follow the Bible! It says how to keep it out. It tells you to kill birds and use their blood, but I couldn't do it! *No faith* −

Beauregard   It's not your fault, madam. It is not your fault −

Mrs Hinchcliffe   If it's him, we must help him. He deserves that. Deserves that kindness . . .

Beauregard   I'm sorry, Mrs Hinchcliffe.

Mrs Hinchcliffe   Please, sir −

Beauregard   I cannot resist the forces at work here! Do you understand? Good day to you.

She sobs.

Mrs Hinchcliffe   Help us!

He goes. Quick black, then light upon the room again. It is late afternoon now. **Florence** *is unconscious upon the floor. The door to the terrace is open and a wind blows flakes of snow.* **Stokes** *bends over her, frantic. He looks around the room. He sees* **Beauregard***'s flask and lifts it to her lips. She coughs, then revives.*

Florence   What's that?

Stokes   Whisky. Beauregard's supplies.

Florence   God.

Stokes   I think they use it to clear ice off the roads in West Virginia.

Florence   He came to me.

Stokes   Beauregard?

Florence   Marchant.

Stokes   What did he want?

Florence   Sir, he did not seem like an older man.

Stokes   Did you see him?

Florence (*shaking her head*)   He was so angry, sir. So lost.

Stokes   Lost? What do you mean?

Florence   This creature, sir, has known no happiness.

Stokes   Elijah Marchant vanished in the East. We know no more . . .

Florence   He craves something now.

Stokes   What?

Florence   Company. Others.

Stokes   Then perhaps we have been gathered here for a reason.

Florence   You believe that?

Stokes   That night upon the landing, you said I had a child.

Florence   It came into my mind.

Stokes   How?

Florence   From yours. For a moment.

Stokes   Florence, I believe you are what spiritualist people call a 'sensitive'. You do possess . . . an *attraction* . . . Perhaps . . . magnetic or . . . electro-biological . . . sympathetic –

Florence   What are you saying, sir?

Stokes   I really have no idea .(*Relief.*) I confess I am quite lost! But that night . . . in the ensuing chaos . . . I . . . held you. And, I am ashamed to say, I −

Florence   You liked it?

Stokes   NO! Lord, no. No, I − Yes. Very much. Please don't think badly of me. But it has been fifteen years since . . . and I promised my wife, you see. I made a promise . . .

Florence   You made a promise to a ghost?

Stokes   No. To . . . a memory. You see, these things, our senses, they can lead us astray . . . not that we are deceived, necessarily, but −

Florence   Sir?

Stokes   Yes.

Florence   I liked it, too.

Stokes   Oh.

Florence   Does God mean us to suffer?

Stokes   To . . . endure . . . perhaps.

Florence   Or to feel?

Stokes   I suppose . . . the literal meaning of the Latin word 'religion' . . . is to rebind, to *rejoin* us to something to −

She kisses him.

Oh good grief, can it mean that?

Florence   I believe it can, sir.

Stokes   I was thinking more of Adam's umbilicus, the −

Florence   Sir, what is your name?

Stokes   My name?

Florence   Your name. First name.

Stokes   It's Gabriel. My mother thought . . . when I was born . . . I had . . . curls, very blond curls and −

Florence   Hello, Gabriel.

Mrs Hinchcliffe (*calls, off*)   Florence!

Florence   I must –

Stokes   Yes . . .

Florence   I should –

Stokes   At once . . .

She exits. He sits, stunned. Fade light on the room and up on the staircase, where **Florence** *meets* **Mrs Hinchcliffe**.

Mrs Hinchcliffe   You brought your boy here?

Florence   No –

Mrs Hinchcliffe   The Professor overturned the house. I've seen his things!

Florence   I couldn't help it, madam.

Mrs Hinchcliffe   This is your fault, girl. You've summoned it. Brought it back!

She hurries off.

Florence   Madam! Listen to me!

Mrs Hinchcliffe (*calls*)   You brought your boy!

Florence   Please!

She follows her.

Black.

Lights have already come up on the room. It is evening. The rear curtains are open. Snow is in the air.

Stokes *is lighting lights, in preparation for a seance.* **Mrs Hinchcliffe** *sits at the table, arms folded, reluctant.*

Stokes   I have asked you here so that we may summon the spirit of Elijah Marchant.

Mrs Hinchcliffe *nods slightly.*

Stokes   You understand?

Another half nod. **Stokes** *sits.*

Mrs Hinchcliffe, I very much appreciate what you told me.

She is silent.

You felt compelled to protect him. His memory.

Mrs Hinchcliffe   It's my livelihood, sir.

Beat.

Stokes   I quite understand.

He lights the final light.

You know it's really quite extraordinary. A Christmas ghost –

Mrs Hinchcliffe   It is Advent, sir. Advent until the bells chime twelve. Then, and only then, does the Saviour enter this world.

Stokes   I apologise.

Beat.

May I ask how you protected yourself from the illness?

Mrs Hinchcliffe   A mask across the mouth. Meals were left at his door. His ablutions were agony for him. I wore gloves, to remove the water and the rags. It took his senses from him, day by day.

Half-beat.

I don't wish for any sort of trouble. I need people to come here. I want it to be a hotel . . .

Stokes   I understand that.

Mrs Hinchcliffe (*looking at the candles*)   Why all these theatrics?

Stokes   I wish I could tell you. But . . . whatever is here . . . it seems to like *this* . . .

Mrs Hinchcliffe   Are you a religious man, Professor?

Stokes   Yes. Absolutely. A sidesman at the chapel at King's –

Mrs Hinchcliffe   You think He'd approve of this?

Stokes   I've no idea. My belief . . . its bedrock . . . is that we are the children of a loving father who would not deceive us . . .

Mrs Hinchcliffe   Faith.

Stokes   Yes.

Mrs Hinchcliffe   Then we must say a prayer.

Stokes   A good idea –

He looks across to the statue of St Francis. It has remained uncovered.

St Francis healing the sick. Specifically, a leper.

Mrs Hinchcliffe   It gave Elijah Marchant comfort.

Stokes   How did I not see?

A knock at the door. **Florence** *enters.*

Florence   Ma'am?

An icy acknowledgement from **Mrs Hinchcliffe**. **Florence** *sits at the table.*

Stokes   Good. I think we are ready to begin.

Mrs Hinchcliffe   The American should be here.

Stokes   But he is not. And I think we are meant to be a circle, aren't we?

He breathes in and exhales, slowly.

And I assume we must join hands . . .

They do so, **Mrs Hinchcliffe** *with great reluctance.*

Beat. Breathing.

Stokes *(calls)*   Is anybody there?

Silence.

(*Awkward.*)   Entities. Things that have no corporeal existence in this world . . . are you among us? (*Sotto.*) Oh Lord . . .

Florence (*sotto*)   Carry on, Gabriel!

Mrs Hinchcliffe *shoots her a look.*

Stokes   Show yourselves . . . please . . .

Mrs Hinchcliffe   Nothing. There'll be nothing.

Stokes   Please . . . send us . . . some greeting . . .

Silence.

Mrs Hinchcliffe   I told you. There'll be nothing to worry about at all −

Suddenly, a door slams, loud. Frantic noise within the house.

Please God, no −

Beauregard *is racing up the stairs.*

Stokes (*marshalling courage*)   Marchant? Elijah Marchant?

Beauregard *explodes into the room by the stage-left door.*

Stokes   BEAUREGARD, YOU DAMNED FOOL!

Beauregard   I'm sorry . . . I'm sorry . . .

Mrs Hinchcliffe (*a half smile*)   I knew you'd come.

Beauregard   Have you begun, Stokes?

Stokes   There was no other choice.

Beauregard   But you don't know what you're doing, man!

He takes his place next to **Florence**.

Stokes   And why the change of heart?

Beauregard (*sotto*)   It exists. Do you concede that it exists?

Stokes   It exists. But why have you −

Beauregard   A debt of honour, sir!

He swigs from his flask. Composes himself.

Stokes (*sotto*)   Are you able to proceed?

Beauregard   I'm ready. Shall I begin?

They join hands again. They settle.

Now. You entities who have no corporeal –

Mrs Hinchcliffe (*sotto*)   He's done that bit!

Florence   Shhh!

Beat.

Beauregard   Elijah Marchant? Are you here? Do you wish to speak with us?

Silence.

Mrs Hinchcliffe   Nothing.

Beauregard   Are you here?

Florence   I think . . . the chance has been lost . . .

Beauregard   There's something.

Stokes   Where?

Beauregard   It's entered the room . . .

Stokes   How do you know?

Beauregard   He is with us.

The candles flicker, almost going out. A storm begins to gather . . .

Elijah Marchant? Tell us. Why do you haunt this place?

Beat.

Why do you haunt this place?

Beat.

Mrs Hinchcliffe (*sotto*)   It isn't him . . .

Beauregard   Elijah Marchant . . .

The storm breaks in the room again. Within it, the voices: 'The Lord is my Shepherd'.

Voices   Please –

I shall not want –

I'll give anything. Please!

He maketh me –

It's coming –

He maketh me –

The wave –

Please God no –

To lie down –

No –

In green pastures –

NO!

Stokes   No . . .

Then silence. **Beauregard** *inhales deeply. He is entranced. He speaks as Bertie, his voice and the child's somehow heard together, utterly different from his impersonation of 'Elizabeth' earlier.*

Beauregard   Papa?

Stokes   Bertie?

Beauregard   It's me, Papa.

Stokes   Beauregard, if this is some trick –

Florence (*whispers*)   He's cold as the grave!

Beauregard   I miss you so much.

Stokes   I miss you, too.

Beauregard   Mama cries.

Stokes   Kiss her for me.

Beauregard It's so dark.

Stokes Find the light.

Beauregard Can't. There's another boy and he won't let me. He won't let me pass . . .

Stokes Who is he?

Beauregard Papa!

Stokes Bertie. WHO IS HE?

Beauregard *exhales suddenly.*

Stokes Bertie? Bertie?

Florence He's gone.

Stokes He can't do that. (*Calls.*) Marchant! Show yourself! GIVE ME MY SON!

Beauregard (*struggling*) Professor, stay calm . . . It wants this . . .

Stokes What does it want? What are you talking about? Give me my child!

A breath, a sigh, within the room.

Florence Was that behind me? It was behind me!

Beauregard Elijah Marchant. Speak!

Florence He's breathing on my neck!

Beauregard Why do you haunt this place?

Florence Help me. Oh, God . . .

Mrs Hinchcliffe (*hissing, sotto*) Shouldn't have begun, should never have begun . . .

Florence He's breathing on me . . . he's . . .

Suddenly, a sound, a blow like that of a great hammer.

Beauregard Jesus!

Mrs Hinchcliffe Please, no . . .

Then the dragging sound that **Stokes** *first heard. Louder, more urgent.*

Stokes   *What is that?*

Beauregard   Elijah Marchant, why are you here? What do you want?

All light is extinguished.

Beat.

Florence (*terrified*)   His hands are on my shoulders!

Stokes   *Who is he?*

Then a knocking all around the room. The windows shake. Objects fall or are thrown around in the dark.

Beauregard   ELIJAH MARCHANT, SPEAK TO US! IN THE NAME OF GOD SPEAK TO US NOW –

Mrs Hinchcliffe   It isn't him. It isn't him. It isn't him . . .

Stokes (*yelling*)   WHO THEN?

Mrs Hinchcliffe   I can't . . .

Stokes   For God's sake, woman, tell us!

Florence *is suddenly poleaxed. She shakes, chokes, as though the breath were being drawn from her. The others stare. She stops.*

When **Florence** *speaks, her voice is that of a boy, about fourteen years of age.*

Beat.

Florence   Hello, Agnes.

Mrs Hinchcliffe   Florence. Stop this.

Florence   You don't recognise me?

Mrs Hinchcliffe   Stop this! (*To* **Stokes**.) Stop her . . .

Stokes   It's not Florence . . .

Mrs Hinchcliffe   Don't talk stupid, of course it's . . .

Stokes   She's a medium!

Mrs Hinchcliffe *moves to shake* **Florence**.

Beauregard   Leave her! She's in a trance!

Mrs Hinchcliffe   She's the girl I took on! The girl I saved from the workhouse, with her mother and the baby –

Florence (*sudden, lengthy, eerie*)   Shhhhh!

Stokes   Spirit, who are you?

Florence (*examining her hands*)   Look. I'm a blackamoor.

Mrs Hinchcliffe (*softer*)   Florence?

Florence   Agnes, look at me.

Beat.

You hadn't the heart to kill the birds. So I killed them.

Beat.

I stopped their little hearts. And I'll stop yours.

For the first time, **Mrs Hinchcliffe** *looks directly at* **Florence**.

Mrs Hinchcliffe   Daniel.

Florence   I've come home, Agnes!

Beauregard (*sotto, to* **Stokes**)   Daniel?

Stokes   Elijah Marchant's son. *Marchant and Son.* No living issue . . .

Florence *turns instantly to* **Stokes**.

Florence   I know you. You want this body.

Stokes   How dare you –

Florence *laughs.*

Mrs Hinchcliffe   Daniel, I did my best for your father . . .

Florence   The disease ate Papa away.

Mrs Hinchcliffe   I'm so sorry . . .

Florence   And we watched. You held me to the glass.

Mrs Hinchcliffe   You could not touch him, Daniel. The risk was too great.

Florence   I wanted to hold him so much.

Mrs Hinchcliffe   He wanted you close. Wanted to see you, but –

Florence   I was a child.

Mrs Hinchcliffe   Daniel, listen to me. The others left. The others ran from this house when they found out about your father. There was no cure, Daniel! No hope. But I stayed, and do you know why I stayed?

Florence   You should have let me in.

Mrs Hinchcliffe   I loved you, Daniel! I loved your father –

Florence   You should have let me in, Agnes.

Mrs Hinchcliffe   I could not! Every day I led you through the house to the glass. And every day you begged to enter the room. *But you could not touch him!*

Beauregard   Daniel? Listen to me. Look to the light.

Florence   What light?

Beauregard   Look!

Florence   It's so cold now.

Stokes   Daniel, why are you here?

Florence   You know why.

Stokes   I don't.

Florence   You called to me.

Mrs Hinchcliffe   Daniel, forgive me if I wronged you . . . but your papa wanted so much to be near you . . . Forgive me!

She leaves the circle, overturning the chair, falls to her knees.

Beauregard   Keep the circle!

Mrs Hinchcliffe   FORGIVE ME!

The room begins to shake, a growing, seismic wave. The table is upturned. **Florence** *stares ahead.*

Beauregard (*to* **Florence**)   Daniel! You're destroying us!

Stokes   What do we do?

Beauregard   I don't know!

Stokes   There must be something!

Beauregard   He can't feel. He needs to *feel*!

Stokes   *Feel? How?*

Beauregard   The thing he loved most he could not hold.
Could not comfort . . .

The noise grows . . .

He believes he cannot feel!

Stokes   Of course he can't, Beauregard! HE'S A GHOST!

Beauregard   Maybe he doesn't know that . . .

Suddenly, **Florence** *is released, falling forward. She struggles to regain herself as . . .*

Daniel Marchant appears at the door, a few steps from the threshold. We see him more clearly. Lost, dishevelled. Drowned.

A bell tolls, distant.

The door opens slowly and without a touch. The glass is suddenly brilliantly illuminated.

Beauregard   Oh God . . .

Mrs Hinchcliffe (*a prayer, rapid, barely audible*)   The Lord is
my Shepherd I shall not want he maketh me he maketh me . . .
The Lord –

Marchant stands, waiting.

Stokes   Daniel?

He stands.

Beauregard   Professor, do not go to him. Professor –

Stokes (*overcome*)   Bertie is with him.

Beauregard   Professor, do not go –

Stokes   He told us!

Florence (*recovering*)   Gabriel?

Stokes   There is a chance to see them again. To be with them again. You must understand . . .

Beauregard   But you cannot –

He moves to stop **Stokes**.

Stokes   I can't be without them any more. It's been so long, so very long to be without them . . .

Beauregard   Listen to me –

Stokes   I have a loss I cannot bear. You had it right before. My life has been *a pale and empty dream*.

Beauregard   But we must live. We must *endure*!

Stokes   No more. Please. No more.

He moves towards the door. **Beauregard** *cannot prevent him.*

Stokes   It's all right, Daniel. There's no need to be alone. There is light –

Florence   No. Oh no please . . .

Stokes   – so much light. Let me show you . . .

Florence   GABRIEL!

Stokes *is on the threshold. He proceeds. As he does so,* **Beauregard** *covers his eyes.*

The door closes behind him

Stokes *embraces Daniel. Daniel responds, clinging to him.*

Florence   Gabriel . . .

Beauregard   Oh sweet Jesus . . .

Mrs Hinchcliffe (*softly*)   Goodbye, child.

Blackout. Silence.

'I Saw Three Ships' sung by a child.

Then . . .

Beauregard (*voice-over*)   And, in conclusion, those are 'The Facts of the Incident at The Sea House'. Christmas Eve, in the Year of Our Lord eighteen hundred and seventy-five. Of my friend, Gabriel Stokes, esteemed writer, Fellow of the Royal Society and Professor of Natural Science at King's College, Cambridge, there has been no word, and no trace. Extensive searches of the house and its grounds, the neighbouring shoreline and the sea itself were hampered by the light and worsening weather conditions upon that Christmas morning. In the absence of a body, Professor Stokes was pronounced dead by a London court six months later. He left no living issue.

Covent Garden. London. Winter 1876. A Christmas tree. The office of **Tom Beauregard**.

Beauregard *is drunk and typing badly. He drinks from a tumbler of whisky. He finishes, takes the sheet of paper and adds it to a manuscript. Clumsily, he shuffles the papers.*

A knock at the door. **Beauregard** *wipes his mouth, attempts to smarten himself up.*

Beauregard   Come!

Florence *enters. She wears a beautiful black dress, her bearing changed.*

Beauregard   Florence!

He rises, unsteady. Kisses her hand.

Well, look at you! The beautiful woman has come. Has it really been a year?

Florence   It has. How are you, Tom?

Beauregard   I'm well. I'm . . . writing. An account of that Christmas. Every fact and detail! You did refer to some news?

Florence   Yes. Agnes Hinchcliffe passed two weeks ago.

Beauregard   She did? Oh, that makes me so sad. She was a good woman. A woman of faith.

Florence   She was mourned, Tom. Many at the funeral.

Beauregard   You know much of my account is based upon her story.

Florence   She endured much.

Beauregard   And so who owns The Sea House now?

Florence   She placed it in trust for Master Caleb Kennedy.

Beauregard   Your son? Congratulations! (*Toasts.*) To Agnes Hinchcliffe! Uh, sorry, you want a drink?

Florence   No. Thank you.

Beauregard *drinks. Becomes self-conscious. Gestures to the manuscript.*

Beauregard   Here it is. 'The Facts of the Incident at The Sea House as witnessed by Thomas Douglas Beauregard the Third, Doctor of the Spiritual Science'. I have publishers interested here and in the United States. Considerable interest, in fact –

Florence   Tom, please don't publish your account.

Beauregard   You know I can't do that.

Florence   I want to make the place a hotel. As Agnes wished, I –

Beauregard   Agnes Hinchcliffe told me everything. How Daniel's mother had died in childbirth, so the boy and his father had been left alone, save for Agnes and a nanny. And when Elijah Marchant returned, sick, the domestics just abandoned the place. But Agnes remained. Daniel would drag his toybox in an impatient rage and hurl abuse at Agnes. But she never faltered. Such was her love for both of them. After Elijah's death, Daniel was sent away to school. But he'd endured too much. No school could hold him. And, at the age of fourteen –

Florence   He drowned himself. I know that part –

Half-beat.

Beauregard   I believe, when Stokes arrived at the house, Daniel sensed a pain as deep as his own. And he reached out. Sure you don't want that drink?

Florence (*with some control*)   Please do not publish.

Beauregard *has a sudden thought. Reaches into his pocket. Produces the apple and sets it upon the table.*

Beauregard   You know, Stokes thought the question of what exists and the incident at The Sea House were different things. But they're the same. All part of the same great *question*. Did the boy exist to Elijah Marchant? By the end . . . did he exist at all?

Florence   Of course he existed!

Beauregard   How? Marchant couldn't *sense*, couldn't see nor feel –

Florence   What do you want me to say? The world exists because it *means* something to us. The other choice is –

Beauregard   Darkness. Cataclysm . . .

Beat.

Florence   Curiouser and curiouser –

Beauregard   What is that?

Florence   A book about a child. A child who gets lost.

Beauregard   Florence, my account of the events at The Sea House will make our names! You and I! I mean to say, you are the finest spirit medium I have ever seen! Imagine what we might achieve *together*!

Florence   You've spent too much time among the spirits, Tom!

Beauregard   But we are upon the edge of such wonders! Don't you see that?

Half-beat.

Florence   Forgive me, but when we first met, you asked if my son were a 'figment' or a 'phantom'. He is neither. Agnes Hinchcliffe saved us through kindness. A simple thing. She gave us warmth, light. Even in death, she gives us a living. If you publish . . . if you put that at risk −

Beauregard (*moved, yet*)   Madam, I have come too far to turn back now −

Florence   Tom −

Beauregard   I have nothing more to say upon this matter. Good day to you.

Half-beat.

Florence   Then I'm sorry. A merry Christmas to you, sir.

She goes.

Beauregard (*calls*)   Matter of fact, it's Advent! Advent till the bells chime twelve!

He drinks. Moves. Sits and addresses **Stokes**'s *seat.*

Beauregard   Professor Stokes, how do we prove a thing exists? How −

A sound, somewhere in the house.

(*Calls.*) Hello? Is anybody there?

Beat.

(*Calls.*) Florence? Florence!

Beat.

Finest spirit medium I have ever seen . . .

He suddenly sits upright.

How do we prove a thing exists, Professor?

He picks up the manuscript.

We prove a thing exists. *We prove a thing exists . . .*

He starts to tear the manuscript.

By ending it.

He tears more pages.

Fade the lights. As they fade we hear 'I Saw Three Ships'.